"Son Husband Father Friend"

Written by: Todd Anthony Hutchinson

First Edition

Copyright © 2026, All Rights Reserved

Published by TKS Venture Holdings, LLC

ISBN# 979-8-999-5244-5-4 (Paperback)

ISBN# 979-8-999-5244-6-1 (e-book)

Book Cover Design by Jana Olivieri

Edited by: Jana Olivieri

No part of this publication may be copied, reproduced in any format, by any means, electronic or otherwise, without prior written consent from the copyright owner and publisher of this book.

Preface

Friendship has always been a crucial aspect in my life. Even though my first 20 years were tough, it was a small group of boys with whom I grew up that had a significant impact on my life. The challenges we faced together, the adventures we went on, and the memories we created will always be a part of me. When I gave my life to Jesus in 1994 and accepted Him as my Savior, it became important to me to grow and mature into a man of God. I had been a worldly man up until that point, and was a runaway train heading off a cliff. As God guided me to read His Word, He began to reveal His purpose and the person He created me to be.

I prayed that wherever He took me, He would also provide me with good men to be around. I knew my weaknesses and understood the Devil would be at my heels, hoping I would return to my old life. It was important to me that I learned how to be a godly man and what that looked like. Over the thirty years since I was saved, God has revealed four areas in my life that I needed to mature in. Those areas were those of a Son, Husband, Father, and Friend. It has been an amazing journey letting the Holy Spirit guide, teach, and correct me in all things masculine.

Now that we live in a world that seems to frown on masculinity and especially moral men, it was time that I wrote down what God had been dealing with in me. I hope this book will be a refresher course for you if you have been walking with the Lord for a while. Maybe you do not have a relationship with Jesus, and your relationship with your father, your spouse, your children, and friends is not as good as you had hoped. My desire is that this book will help you build a proper foundation for being a mature man in Christ.

It is a journey to find your true, authentic, spiritual self. To come to the knowledge and understanding of who God created you to be. There will be highs and lows. Bumps and bruises. In the end, as God refines us all, we will hopefully begin to look closer to His image than ours. Enjoy the four masculine archetypes we discuss, and the four pillars attached to each archetype. Write things down! Highlight words and sentences that speak to your soul and spirit. Above all, submit yourself to God's grace and allow Him to shape your heart to His design. Hopefully, this will encourage you to be a better man! That is all we can hope for. Let us be the example, let us lead the charge. God Bless! Let's start your journey!

Contents

Chapter 1 Male Spiritual Archetypes 9

Chapter 2 Your Adoption as a Son 20

Chapter 3: Being a Godly Husband 35

Chapter 4 Father Foundations 51

Chapter 5 Friends Stick Closer than a Brother 69

Chapter 6 Become a Mature Man 87

Chapter 7 Make Disciples 93

Chapter 1 Male Spiritual Archetypes

As I author this book in the Fall of 2025, it is plainly obvious through my spiritual eyesight that the horrors of Romans 1:18-32 and 2 Timothy 3:1-9 are unfolding. The beginning of open and programmed lawlessness is in full force. I am aware that, as Solomon wrote in Ecclesiastes 1:9, "there is nothing new under the sun." We are on a collision course with the inevitable end of the age, according to the Book of Revelation. Since time began on our *terra firma* and Sin entered the world through Adam, man's struggle to return to his original design has been a constant battle.

We are bombarded on all sides, especially in this new millennium, with every fleshly desire available to us 24 hours a day, seven days a week, through our personal devices. The last-ditch effort of Satan to destroy the four spiritual archetypes of men is in full force. There has been a slow societal decay of the strength of a Godly man. The uprooting of the four progressive journeys God had ordained for man. The natural maturing process of becoming **a son, a husband, a father, and a friend.**

These four fundamental and foundational archetypes have been under fire since the Garden of Eden. In the last 50 years, we have seen a slow dismantling of man, especially in the United States of America. It began with the education system, which was built on fundamental historic and spiritual truths and was replaced with the demonic and destructive focus on humanism and self-worship.

That was followed by the destructive welfare and abortion movements, which ripped a gaping hole in the nuclear family and began rewarding women to raise children with no father in the house or to abort future children of God. Child sacrifice is nothing new; it is the continued worship of the god Moloch, who is the demonic god of child sacrifice. A tradition that has been active for thousands of years. The rate of divorce skyrocketed, and broken homes became the norm rather than the minority.

The next onslaught was the sexual revolution, where homosexuality became a programmed psyop designed to reduce and eliminate the importance and the role of the heterosexual male figure. This was by far the largest and most organized programming designed by Satan. Movies, television shows, songs, and commercials began to deify the male in societal norms and started showing him in the most negative lights as possible.

Now, as Solomon explained earlier, there is nothing new under the sun. Homosexuality has been around since *The Watchers* came down and manipulated the Children of God. The Book of Enoch, in detail, describes the knowledge that was given by the Sons of God to man and how manipulative and detrimental it was to society.

God has dealt with this Sin for thousands of years. While Satan programmed same-sex intercourse into the mainstream consciousness as something normal or God-forbid, even innate at birth, as Romans and 2 Timothy clearly state, God abhors the behavior. Now, for those who have rejected God and have embraced Satan as their lord, this behavior is a foundation in their rituals and practices. From the pure religion of Satanism to Cults such as Free Masons, Skull & Bones Societies,

Hollywood elites, and many others, Sodomy is a rite of passage and required.

The next and current design of Satan to destroy Man's relationship with God is the Technological Era. From the beginning of the internet to the World-Wide push of social media and handheld devices connected to the World Wide Web, man has complete access to every dark corner available to destroy himself. You see it everywhere you go. Men and women are together, but their heads are down, looking at their devices. The physical engagement through dialogue and presence has been replaced by texting and social media communication.

The final weapon to destroy the Spiritual Archetypes of men is the 24-hour access to porn. A large majority of men have forsaken their Spiritual relationship with God, their wife, and their children and given their attention, desire, and energy to watching porn. This weapon has destroyed marriages, relationships, and men's true calling in life, which is to be a God-honoring son, husband, father, and friend.

The true weapon of Satan is to create the illusion that politics is the truth. To supplant God's authority over your life and replace it with a president, a congressman, or a local official. Giving them power and authority over your life and above the authority of Scripture. Romans 13:1 and 1 Peter 2:13-14 are clear in their instruction to respect and honor those God has put in power. It does not, though, inform us to blindly follow what they are selling.

Recently, the demonically controlled media has created the psyop of the "Evil White Male" and the false truth of "White-Privilege." These two brainwashing assignments are in full force through the education system, the political system, and the Hollywood system. All is a designed effort to attack and chop down the male spiritual archetypes of Husband and Father. Satan fears the authority and position of a man who has submitted to the Authority of Jesus Christ and is on a journey to become like Christ in every area of his life. Satan hates this so much that he has begun a full assault on these archetypes and wants the world to be convinced that a strong, healthy, spiritual Husband and Father is the enemy of society.

The dangerous 'Alpha-Male" that is there to destroy society. The "Alpha-Male" is dangerous, racist, homophobic, gender phobic, anti-immigration, anti-women's rights, anti-equal rights, and much more. You cannot open up social media or watch television without seeing programmed episodes and shorts designed to show men in a negative light. To show them as weak and ineffective. If you have ears to hear and eyes to see, Satan's plan has been abundantly clear for the last five decades. Now we have arrived where weak, confused, idol-worshipping, and cause-worshipping men are the ones put front and center on the news, and public eye.

Now, are there "Alpha-Males" that resemble the above-mentioned behavior? Absolutely. Are they all "white?" No? Racism, bigotry, and abuse come in all shapes and colors. These behaviors are a result of self-will running rampant. The Bible has clear instructions on how to love your neighbor and your wife, so men who behave in such a poor manner toward others and their spouse are not adhering to biblical principles, which we will discuss in this book.

What does Satan want? He wants men not to love and serve God. He wants them to marry a man so they cannot procreate. He does not want them to be fathers or raise Godly men. He wants them angry, unhappy, and slaves to him for their entire life. Unfortunately, more and more, he is succeeding. Even in modern day Churches, where Godly men are supposed to be encouraged, mentored, and built up, we see a wave of adultery, divorce, and even, recently, a resurgence in pedophilia inside the church.

This is all a result of men refusing the four Spiritual Archetypes of God and succumbing to their fleshly desires and lusts. Worshiping the creation and not the Creator (Romans 1:25). In this book, we will discuss the four Spiritual Archetypes God has designed for man. One, that of a **Son**. The designed relationship between God and Adam, which was created out of the original relationship of the Godhead, Jesus Christ, the Son, and God, the Father. The importance of understanding your adoption of a son to God through the sacrifice of Jesus Christ, the Son of God.

The next Archetype is that of a **Husband**. Understanding the designed role of Man to marry a woman, procreate, and provide for his family. Understanding the authority of the groom, as Jesus himself is the groom and the church is his bride. The spiritual power and blessing that come with being a faithful husband and partnering with a woman to grow in Christ together.

The third archetype we will discuss is the role of a **Father**. The roadmap of learning how to allow God to be your spiritual father, so you can be mentored by the Holy Spirit to raise your children biblically and spiritually that brings honor to God. Creating a foundation for your children to be mature and successful in their future.

The fourth archetype we will discuss is the role of a **Friend**. Understanding the importance of biblical friendship and community. How we are one body, fully equipped to do the work of God. Each of us is designed with our own gifts and talents and made to fit perfectly with others to advance the Gospel of Jesus to the world as the day of His return approaches.

My hope is that spiritual men and women read this book and return their attention to the Bible and what it has to say about being a good son, husband, father, and friend. For anyone who does not have a relationship with God but can see that the principles designed to govern and grow man in a healthy and productive way for himself, others, and society come from God himself.

We will discuss hard truths like how sin is a destroyer of good men and women. How society has grown increasingly separated and desperate because of our pursuit of selfish desires. We will discuss how the repentance of evil men and their turning back to God can and will create a better world for everyone. The path that we are on now will only accelerate into more chaos and division. If everyone is serving themselves, society fails. I hope this small book is a blessing to you. I hope it reminds you how important it is to believe in and have a relationship with God, as well as emphasize that your desires *can* be fulfilled in a righteous and generational way when you follow after Him.

Hopefully, if you find yourself falling short in these four areas, you can repent, change your heart, and attempt to be a better man in the future. May God, give you grace and wisdom to follow your spiritual heart and fall in love with Him again. To become the man, He created you to be. To fulfill the purpose and destiny He designed for you. For you to no longer serve Satan and your flesh, but to understand the eternal reward of becoming a son of God!

Let us begin our journey!

Chapter 2 Your Adoption as a Son

One of the largest dilemmas in society today, if not the largest dilemma, is the overwhelming number of children being raised in a fatherless home. Whether it is a child born out of wedlock to an absent father or young children living through the divorce of their parents and getting only a few days a month with the father. My story, which began in the early seventies, was the same. My father and mother divorced when I was one, and from there my mother got married twice, so I had two stepfathers to contend with. The absence of one stable male figure in the home does an immense amount of visible and invisible damage to a child's soul and spirit, especially young men. It unfortunately creates a pattern that a young man will more than likely repeat as he grows.

The importance of having one stable father cannot be underestimated. Someone who is there to teach you proper instructions for life, how to treat others, how to work hard for the things you desire, and how to become a stable male figure in your future. The good news is we have an Abba Father who is the Alpha and Omega and is omnipresent. God the Father, who is the Creator and Father of all things. I never understood the importance of being a son until 1994, when I gave my life to Jesus, accepted Him as Savior and Lord of my life, and began to read the Word of God.

Growing up with little guidance from my father, whom I rarely saw, and stepfathers burdened by their own struggles, I lacked the teaching I needed to understand how to be a good son and what my role should be. The unfortunate result was 23 years of me questioning who I was, being afraid to be honest about my emotions, or being uncomfortable asking for help. For many young men raised without a present father, maturity is stunted, and it may take years—or never—for them to grasp the vital importance of that role. God created man to have fellowship with Him. Both men and women were designed to have a Creator and Father in God. He should always be our first counsel. The source that provides us with wisdom, discernment, maturity, confidence, and grace. In the Bible, Jeremiah 1:5 states that *"Before I formed you in the womb, I knew you."* I love this proclamation from God. It explains that before our Father and Mother conceived us, God planned for us to exist. All He needed was two people to physically make it happen. This confirms and destroys the myth that anyone is an accident. It confirms that our Spirit and Soul were created before our physical body was conceived in the natural realm.

Before Jena and Larry provided sperm and egg to create a physical version of me, God and I were already in conversation about when and where I would live my physical life. This should give you great comfort in knowing that, despite who your parents are or how you were conceived, you and God had already planned your arrival.

My first spiritual role is to be a son. To honor my father and mother is a physical and spiritual mandate. Now, the moment you are physically born into this fallen world, you are bombarded by the principalities, powers, demons, Devils, and rulers of this world. Because of this, finding Jesus as your Lord and Savior as early as you can is beneficial. I had 23 years of battling the forces of evil and human error until I accepted Christ as Savior and understood I had spiritual weapons, tools, and the Holy Spirit to defend myself against evil.

Believe me, the Devil made many attempts on my life growing up. There were many situations I look back at now and wonder how I escaped that.

Now, some will bring up Romans 8:29 and discuss predestination and foreknowledge, and that may be the case, but that is for another book, not this one. The truth is, I came to Christ kicking and screaming like most people. It took an ex-drug dealer who invited me to church for over a year. I was living a good life, early twenties, lead singer in an original rock band in Orlando, Florida. My life consisted of working at TGI Friday's, band rehearsal, performing, and partying. 'Wine, Women and Song,' as the songs and books infer.

On the surface, I seemed happy and that I was living my best life. Only God knew on the inside that I was in utter ruins. I still had not dealt with the death of my mother that happened a few years back. I had no mentor or father figure in my life, shaking me and giving me guidance. My life consisted of work, partying, sleep, and repeat. I treated women like objects, and I treated my friends like they were ornaments to make me look better than I was. I was an absolute mess and had lost my understanding of being a son of the Highest.

Romans 8:14-17 states that *"For those who are led by the Spirit of God are the* **children of God**. *The Spirit you received does not make you slaves, so that you live in fear again; rather, the Spirit you received brought about your* **adoption to sonship**. *And by him we cry,* **"Abba, Father."** *The Spirit himself testifies with our spirit that we are* **God's children**. *Now if we are children, then we are heirs—heirs of God and co-heirs with Christ, if indeed we share in His sufferings so that we may also share in His glory."*

This was one of the first books I read, as recommended by my new ex-drug-dealer friend. After I finally succumbed to his leading to come to church, it was there that I heard a powerful message and was led by the Holy Spirit to go to the altar and accept Jesus's love and sacrifice. He gave me a Bible and suggested that I start with The Gospel of John and the Book of Romans.

I remember late at night in my room reading these passages and others and understanding that what I had been wanting my whole life, a stable, full-time, loving Father, had always been available to me in the form of God. 'Abba Father!' I wanted to be a son! I wanted to have that loving father who was there for everything and had the words I needed to hear. I continued to eat the

Word of God. When I was not at work, rehearsal, or performing, I was at a coffee shop somewhere with my Bible. Reading passages like Galatians 4:4-7 *"But when the set time had fully come, God sent His Son, born of a woman, born under the law, to redeem those under the law, that we might* **receive adoption to sonship**. *Because you are* **His sons**, *God sent the Spirit of* **His Son into our hearts**, *the Spirit who calls out,* **"Abba, Father."** *So, you are no longer a slave, but* **God's child**; *and since you are* **His child**, *God has made you also* **an heir**.*"*

The disappointment of the imperfect fathers I had was now replaced with a perfect, loving, and present Father in God Almighty. I began to understand that God had always been the Father figure, and He and I had had a relationship before I came into this world. *"For He chose us in Him before the creation of the world to be holy and blameless in His sight. In love He* **predestined us for adoption to sonship** *through Jesus Christ, in accordance with His pleasure and will."* Ephesians 1:4-5 confirmed. Now that I had accepted Jesus as Lord, my spiritual adoption as a son could now manifest in my life.

This changed everything for me. I had never felt completely loved, like the way I now felt loved and affirmed by Jesus and God the Father. His Word began to confirm the love that was bestowed upon me, and the instructions of who I was to be became clear. Now I know there will be those who are reading this who had a wonderful father in their life. Perhaps you grew up with both father and mother who are still married. Most likely, your dad loved you and provided all that you needed to the best of his ability. If that is the case for you, I will suggest that your father was able to do that because he either had the same or, at some point in his life before creating you, he understood what it was to be a son of God.

So, what does it mean to be a son of God? To be a good son? To fulfill the first calling in this life? I will give you four pillars that you must construct and keep on the foundation of God's word. The first pillar or role of a son is to **worship and honor God!** The first and fifth commandments in the Bible are from Exodus. *"You shall have no other gods before Me."* The fifth states, *"Honor your Father and Mother."* This one comes with a blessing of long life.

In a nutshell, it means do not put anything before or higher than your love for God. As we go into the other roles of Husband, Father, and Friend, this applies as well under those roles. As I took on the roles of husband, father, and friend, the same truth held whatever discord or distrust I felt toward my father or stepfathers, I still had to honor their place in my life—even when I disagreed with how they raised me or expressed affection. I honored the fact that God had placed them over me for His purpose. Even those fathers who abuse their children. You do not excuse abusive behavior, and you avoid contact with them if that is what is required.

Giving honor means not to publicly slander them and expose them. We remember the story of Noah and his boys when they finally landed after the waters of the great flood had subsided (Genesis 9). Noah planted a vineyard, decided to get drunk and naked. When Ham found him, instead of covering him up and not exposing his condition, he ran to the other sons and exposed his father's shame. He did not honor Noah, his father. Shem and Japheth took a garment and covered him. They honored their father.

The second pillar and role of a son is to **Seek Wisdom and the Knowledge of God's Word.** Proverbs 1 & 2 give clear and concise instructions on how to seek, obtain, and retain wisdom and knowledge. It also goes over the benefits of wisdom and knowledge. In fact, the Book of Proverbs is one of the best books to study as a Son, Husband, Father and Friend. Written by Solomon, who God blessed to be one of the wisest men to ever live (1 Kings 4:29-30).

At twenty-three, I had plenty of worldly knowledge and wisdom. I lived for my flesh. I was incredibly selfish. I consciously and subconsciously hurt anyone who stood in my way or whom I didn't like. I was on what AC/DC called a *Highway to Hell*. An excellent riff by the way. When I gave my life to the Lord and began reading the Word of God, my life began to change. I gained Godly wisdom and knowledge. The Holy Spirit began to show me where I had fallen short, how I had been treating myself and others. God poured out on me his loving grace and gave me the power and opportunity to better myself through his word.

The third Pillar or Role as a son is to **Be at Peace with Yourself and with Others**. Matthew 5:9 confirms this as Jesus Himself proclaims, *"Blessed are the peacemakers, for they will be called sons of God."* This has everything to do with understanding your identity in Christ Jesus and who God has called you to be. We struggle in this world, balancing what the world wants us to become or claims we should become versus what God's word says about us. We see this ever so clearly in today's world as we are going through identity dysphoria and identity politics. The LGBT+ and transgender movements strike at the very heart of what and who God says we are.

The Devil has convinced hundreds of millions of people that their nature, identity, and physical design can change anytime they want and as many times as they want. It gives the proverbial middle finger to God and His truth that He made us male and female, and that we are made in His image. The enemy of the soul whispers that identity can be as fluid as however or wherever one's emotions might go. That ideology and thought process destroys the very solid foundation that God created for us for a purpose and truth, and that you are made perfect in His image (Genesis 1:27). That you were fearfully and wonderfully made (Psalm 139:14).

Unless your identity is rooted firmly in who God says you are, the world will do everything in its power to destroy you and pull you as far away from the truth as possible. Eventually, you become so confused that you eventually self-destruct, which is the Devil's plan. The suicide rate in the LGBT+ and trans community is Satan's design. If you want to know who you are, your gifts and callings, and your divine purpose in life, all that comes from spending time with God, the Holy Spirit, and reading His words. Finding who you are and understanding your role and calling as a son will give you the wisdom and respect to give to others. You will understand the calling God has on their life. You will begin to treat them as brothers and sisters in God and do your best to lift them, encourage them, and when necessary, rebuke them in Love as the Holy Spirit instructs.

The fourth Pillar or Role as a son is **to show other men how to be Sons!** Jesus, as he ascended into Heaven, gave final instructions to the disciples. *"Therefore, go and* *make disciples of all nations, baptizing them in the name of the Father and of the Son and of the Holy Spirit, and teaching them to obey everything I have commanded you. And surely, I am with you always, to the very end of the age."* Jesus spoke these words, and it was recorded in Matthew 28:19-20. As I gave my life to Jesus and began to worship and honor Him as Lord, he gave me a desire to read the Word of God and gain understanding of who He is. As I gained knowledge about who God was and is, it gave me an understanding of who I was. My identity in Him became a solid foundation for me. I began to make choices that were beneficial for my growth and maturity based on the biblical truths I was consuming. Many of the false beliefs and worldly principles I had built my life on were being debunked and stripped away.

I began to live my life according to God's purpose and calling for me. This did not mean I didn't stumble, sin, or make mistakes. I was still human. It just meant I had the understanding and wisdom to seek God, repent, and allow the Holy Spirit to strengthen me. As I grew in my stature as a son of God, my final role was to show others what a difference it had made in my life. Most people refer to this as your testimony. How did I go from being a reckless, drunk, liar, womanizer, and idolator, to being a faithfully married man who puts God in the center of all his choices? It was coming into my role as a son of the Highest. Most had read about the Prodigal Son (Luke 15:11-32), who devalued his position, asked for all his reward now, and proceeded to squander everything. When he found himself in the mud with the pigs, he realized whose son he was and what it meant to be the son of such a man. He repented and returned.

Once I understand my position and authority as a son of God, it is my duty to make sure that light shines bright enough for others who walk in darkness and unbelief to be able to see and be drawn to (Matthew 5:16). That includes family members, friends, coworkers, and those who God puts in my path. Like I said, will I make mistakes? Yes! But because I have God's word in me, I repent, retie my running shoes, and finish my race. I have consistently, for the last two decades did what I call "Grown Ass Men's" nights. It is when I host an event where 6-12 men show up, we eat, talk, and fellowship together. I usually have a topic to discuss that I know most men deal with. As a group, we share our experiences and discuss how God has given us the grace and tools to become better men.

In review, on becoming a Son. Understand that God sent His own son, Jesus, to be the sacrifice for us, so that we, through Him, may come boldly to the throne of God. From there, it is our journey to become sons by

1)Worshiping and honoring God.

2)To seek his Wisdom and the Knowledge of God's Word.

3)To **Be at Peace with Yourself and with Others.**

4)To **Show other Men how to be Sons.**

One of the main obstacles in being the next role in God's Kingdom, that of a Husband, is those who get married before they have understood their role as a son.

I recommend you study every verse in the Bible that has to do with sonship. Take your time and let God fill you with His Fatherly love. In the next chapter, we will discuss the next role in our lives, in God's will, and that is the role of being a Godly Husband.

Let us continue our journey!

Chapter 3: Being a Godly Husband

In 2026, my wife and I will be celebrating 27 years of marriage. The odds of us surviving when we got married were not good. I am sure all our friends were happy for us on that day, but if they were being truthful, many of them didn't believe it would last. Let's face it, over fifty percent of us have grown up in broken homes, so the idea of a lifelong marriage seems wonderful—but the reality is that over half of marriages these days end up in divorce. A year before I got married, I had been planning to move to Los Angeles with one of my best friends and pursue my dream of being a screenwriter, actor, and filmmaker. We had made our plans and saved our money. About six months before we were planning on moving, my wife saw us in a bar in San Antonio and came to sit with us. 'The rest is history,' as they say.

Two months later, we got engaged, and two months after that, we were married. My friend moved to Los Angeles and has enjoyed a successful career out there. The Bible says, "*Whosoever finds a wife, finds a good thing, and obtains favor from the Lord.* (Proverbs 18:22)" Proverbs 31:10 adds to that and says, *"Who can find a virtuous woman? Her price is far above rubies!"*

I am so blessed to find a virtuous and great woman in my wife. I wish I could have said I was prepared for marriage, but I was twenty-seven. I still had some maturing to go on with how to be a godly husband, so the first 10-12 years were full of painful growth. I wish more fathers or pastors would spend more time with young men to discuss the foundations of being a godly husband, but who am I kidding? Most of those young men wouldn't listen anyway. Some things must be learned the hard way; it is the only thing that sticks.

I wanted to give you some wisdom on the now 27 years of being a husband and what the Word of God says about being a husband. I recommend you do a search for yourself and dig into the scriptures to get a foundation as well. I am going to provide you with four pillars to build on to be a godly husband.

The four pillars are:

1) Make Christ the Head.

2) Love in Wholeness and Honor.

3) Provide and Decide.

4) **Stand in the Gap.**

These four pillars, if done in humility and grace, God willing, will create a firm structure to build a great marriage and provide a stable home to raise children and grandchildren as well. Whether you are single, about to get married, or a decade into a rocky marriage, hopefully this will help you become the husband God desires you to be.

The first pillar is to **Make Christ the Head** of your marriage. 1 Corinthians 11:3 states, *"But I would have you know that the head of every man is Christ, and the head of the woman is man, and the head of Christ is God."* This scripture gives a clear rank and file of how authority and responsibility should flow in a godly marriage. God is the Almighty. Sitting at the right hand of God is Jesus. Christ is the head of the man, and the man is the head of the woman or wife. As a godly husband guided by

God, it is your authority and responsibility to then guide your wife into a relationship with God. When tough decisions are to be made, it is your responsibility to pray and get with God on the right decisions.

The spiritual temperature of the home should begin with the husband. Men, especially those who claim to have a relationship with God, the evidence should be clear. The time you spend with God in your prayers and reading God's word should be evident in your everyday life. I remember for four years I had a job that was a 45-minute commute every morning and longer every afternoon. The job was stressful, and when I was home, my brain was fried. My good wife, for Christmas, bought me the New Testament on CD (I'm dating myself, ha-ha!)

Till this day, that was one of the best gifts I ever received. For years, my commute back and forth from work, I would listen repeatedly to the entire New Testament on those CD's. It made my commute seem less cumbersome, and I began to devour and retain the Word of God, especially the gospels and Jesus's teachings. As I grew stronger in the word, I began to let Jesus guide me in all wisdom, and I began to make smarter and more spiritually guided decisions for our household. Not all of them felt good, but they were guided by the Holy Spirit.

As I stepped into my authority, with Jesus as my head and covering, He began to guide me in making decisions that blessed my family's life. In my career, financially, physically, and most importantly, spiritually. My wife and I's relationship became stronger. Many of the little things that would trigger a disagreement, or fight began to be solved and went away. My wife and I begin every morning with coffee, reading the word and then praying together. Every decision regarding our finances, physical health, children, and future, we sit down and discuss. Ultimately, I must be the one who decides on which direction we will go by listening to the Holy Spirit and submitting myself to Christ's authority.

Do I get everything right? No! Does God allow me to make mistakes? Yes! Sometimes I miss it. I miss Him! When that happens, I repent, seek His Face, and pray for grace! Being the head of the house is an incredibly challenging position. Not everyone and not every decision will feel good. But to be a Godly husband, you need to put on your 'Big-Boy-Pants' every day and seek God's wisdom.

The second pillar is **Love in Wholeness and Honor**. Ephesians 5:25 states, *"Husbands, love your wives, even as Christ loved the Church and gave His life for it."* Ephesians 5:28 continues in that vein and states, *"So ought men to love their wives as their own bodies. He that loves his wife, loves himself."* This is very similar to the 'Golden Rule' or when Jesus said that the law can be summed up in two things, *"Love the Lord your God with all your heart and with all your soul and with all your mind and with all your strength. The second is 'love your neighbor as yourself.' There is no commandment greater than these.* (Matthew 12:30-31)"

Husbands who are abusive to their wives do so because they hate themselves. If we are to be like Christ, then our love for our wives should be like His love for us. We should be willing to lay down our lives for them. Not that Christ will demand that, but it should always be a conviction in your heart. It means to show honor to your wife. Have respect for her as your spouse and the mother of your children. Colossians 3:19 states, *"Husbands love your wives and be not bitter against them."* Do not be harsh, raise your voice, be violent with them, belittle them, or provoke them to anger. Husbands should be gentle, kind, and steadfast with their faith and support.

The very first union in the Bible in Genesis 2:24 stated, *"Therefore shall a man leave his father and mother and shall cleave unto his wife, and they shall become one flesh."* God had created man and woman to be in union. Woman was created by the very bone of man, so woman is created by our own flesh and bone. This is why it is unnatural to abuse or mistreat a woman; it is akin to abusing and mistreating yourself. 1 Corinthians 7:3 states, *"Let the husband render unto the wife due benevolence; and likewise, also the wife unto the husband."*

Do not hold back your affection from each other, especially the wife. This includes all things: communication, love, encouragement, physical affection and touch, respect, and faithfulness. Be respectful to each other's bodies, minds, and spirits. There should be no forced affection or attention. Many ungodly men have been known to abuse scripture for their physical needs; this is abhorrent to God.

The union between a godly man and woman, with Christ in the center of all things, is designed to last and be strong. Ecclesiastes 4:12 states, *"A person standing alone can be attacked and defeated, but two can stand back-to-back and conquer. Three are even better, for a triple-braided cord, is not easily broken."* This speaks of the strong and God-ordained unity of the marriage union between a man and a woman with Christ as the head of that union. A godly husband first loves the Lord with all his heart, soul, mind, and strength. He loves himself because of that. Now he can love his wife with the same faith and vigor.

Whether you are married now or about to consider marriage, it is not too late to recommit your faith and become a godly husband. Paul in 1 Corinthians 7:7-8 states, *"For I would that all men were even as I myself. But every man hath his proper gift of God, one after this manner, and another after that. I say therefore to the unmarried and widows, it is good for them if they abide even as I."* He does advise, especially to men, that if God has given you the grace to be single and give your life to the service of serving God, then do so. Desiring to be married comes with the responsibility of being a godly husband and leading a family by faith and Holy Spirit-led guidance. It is not for the faint of heart.

The third Pillar for a godly husband is to **Provide and Decide**. 1 Timothy 5:8 states, *"But those who won't care for their relatives, especially those in their own household, have denied the true faith. Such people are worse than unbelievers."* This is as basic as it gets. If you plan on being a husband and starting a family, then it is your responsibility to provide for that wife and family. Does this mean you have to be a millionaire? No! It means you need to maintain a steady job or own a business that provides the basic needs for you and your family. God never intended man to be lazy. He gave us all the physical and mental skills to create wealth.

Have I lost a job while being married? Yes. I quickly found another one or took two part-time jobs to pay for the bills and provide food on our table. I found myself waiting tables in my twenties, thirties, forties, and yes, even fifties when needed. It is my responsibility to provide for my family. Does that mean my wife stays home? If God provides for that, and if she is called to do that. I have friends whose wives have also stayed home and raised the children, and God provided through the husband all their needs. I have friends whose wives work, and the two incomes provide for all the needs. Not all women want to stay home; some have a desire to work and earn a living as well.

These decisions need to be made in the courting process before rings are put on fingers. Has my wife stayed home and did not work? Yes, for a few years, God provided enough for me to handle. Sometimes, where you live makes a difference as well. I grew up in small towns in Florida, where the cost of living is affordable. My wife and I raised our son just north of Dallas, TX, in one of the fastest-growing areas in the United States. The cost of living here keeps going higher. We made the decision that it was worth raising our child in good school districts and a safe environment. So, when I had to work two jobs, I did.

As a godly husband, it is my role to provide and make hard decisions. One of those decisions I made in 2010. My wife and I in 2005 made a mistake that many people made back then and are making today. We bought a house during the housing boom. We spent about 25%

more than we should have. It was a fantastic house in a pristine area. It was a great place to raise our son. But as the economy struggled, gas, food, and living expenses went up, and we began to struggle to barely make it. We both lost our jobs, and we got into a position where we used our credit cards more than we should. I had a decision to make, and it was a hard one. I had gotten a new job that paid me well.

The new job would allow my wife to stay home and spend more time with our son, who was in middle school. It would mean, though, that we would have to downsize from the house. A decision, neither one of us wanted to make, but the pressure of keeping up with the Joneses was about to ruin our marriage. I had to make the hard choice to downsize and allow my wife to stay home. As Cuba Gooding Jr. said in *Jerry Maguire*, "It's not sexy!" It wasn't a sexy choice, but it made all the difference in the world. My wife stayed home. She spent more time with our son. She spent more time with the Lord and her friends, and it reaped a great harvest in her.

We spent two years rebuilding and were able to get back into an affordable house just before our son started High

School. I was providing what we needed, on a scaled-down version, but we were happier. Sometimes we put ourselves in a position where we take on too much, thinking that it will last. Life finds a way to disrupt our plans. Having a strong relationship with God as a godly husband will give you the wisdom and grace to make tough, but righteous decisions for your family. Providing and making hard decisions leads us into the fourth pillar for being a godly husband, which is **Standing in the Gap**. Being the Good Shepherd and protecting the flock from the ravenous wolves of life!

As Jesus proclaimed, He was the Good Shepherd. The Shepherd who guards the sheep. Keeping wolves, lions, and other predators from getting to the sheep. As a godly husband, that is your role. As we have seen in the last decade or so, social media and social agendas have blanketed our lives. From the television airways to all the social media platforms, we devour daily from our devices. As the head of the household and the protector, you must keep a vigilant watch on what is brought into the home. Ezekiel 22:30 God was looking for a strong man to stand in the gap and protect the nation. God is looking for these types of men and will bless them and equip them as they stand.

This includes what you allow to enter into your consciousness as well. Since the public access to computers and the internet, the porn epidemic has become a massive Tsunami rolling over the lives of countless millions for decades now. It has even infected the Church and Christians in large numbers. The predator and demon that is porn has caused an increase in the number of divorces, adultery, and, horrifically, an uptick in pedophilia. In the last few years, we have seen a large number of pastors step down and even be arrested for heinous, sexually lewd acts. These were supposed to be godly men, setting a standard for Christian men all over the world and standing in the gap against such things. Because they were not diligent and forgot their role, they fell victim to the Devil and his trickery.

As a godly husband, it is your charge to have a consistent and powerful relationship with God. To be the standard set in the home. The pressure is high! The stress is continuous! God put the mantle on men to be that strong tower, that fortress of refuge for the home, just like He is for you. What does it mean to stand in the gap? Be awake! Stay watch! Carry your Rod and Staff with you at all times. Men need to stay in the world continually. Pray fervently. Keep your eyes and ears open to what the Lord is doing.

The Devil will send every distraction possible to keep you away from your task. That can be sending you a "love for money," a wandering eye for other women, a spirit of laziness, or attack your health through bad eating and not being active. So many ways you can be attacked as a Godly man. Ephesians 6:10-18 should be a man's best friend. Understanding that every day we need to wake up, put on the armor of God, pray for our families and ourselves, and understand that we do not battle against flesh and blood, but principalities, powers and rulers of the air.

In review, as you pray and desire to be a Godly husband keep these four pillars at the forefront of your mind, heart and Spirit. Make Christ the Head! Love your wife in Wholeness and Honor! Provide for your wife and be ready to make tough decisions when needed! Be ready and equipped to Stand in the Gap for your wife, being fully equipped and armed for the attacks of the enemy. This is the second masculine role God has ordained for men. The next role we will discuss is the role of a Godly Father! In Genesis 1:28 God commanded them 'to be fruitful and multiply.' It is God's design for a man to find a woman, to make her his wife and for the two of them to be joined and produce children. In the next chapter we will discuss being a Godly father and the pillars of that role.

Let us continue our journey!

Chapter 4 Father Foundations

As we progress through the four masculine archetypes God has designed for men, we now come to one of the most crucial in today's world, the role of a **Father**! Most psychologists and psychiatrists will agree that the number one factor destroying our societies today is the absence of stable father figures in the home. According to a study done by the America First Policy Institute, a survey done in 2024 revealed that the United States has the highest rate of children in single-parent households of any nation in the world. They also revealed that there are over 18 million fatherless children in the U.S.

Other stats continued in stating that fathers are absent from 80% of single-parent homes, fatherless families are 4x more likely to live in poverty than that of married couple families, fatherless children are more likely to abuse drugs and show signs of delinquent behavior, and 70% of juveniles in state-operated institutions come from single-parent households. These alarming numbers will only rise as society has become more and more against the nuclear family, especially those who are guided by a faith-filled father.

This is a glaring example of why this trend needs to end as quickly as possible and why men need to become the Spirit-filled, mighty men of God that he designed from the beginning. The four pillars of a father's foundation that we will discuss in this chapter are:

1) Spiritual leader.

2) A Strong Tower and Storehouse.

3) A Role Model.

4) A Generational Builder.

These pillars will continue to build the strong house that began with being a son and husband. First and foremost, a father must be a **Spiritual leader**! A man whose faith is in the Lord Jesus Christ and whose lips can call out 'Abba Father' on every occasion. An upright man, filled with integrity, compassion, wisdom, and love,

I could write an entire other book on what a Jezebel Spirit has done to destroy Spiritual men in this world. Let's just say that that spirit has an ocean full of blood following in her wake. As a father, with the responsibility of raising the next generation of men and women, it is imperative to have a foundation built on the truth of the Word of God. To have a clear and unwavering understanding of the difference between right and wrong. To discern wickedness the moment it raises its eyes in your family's direction. To have the weapons and a soldier's instinct to attack and defend your own.

As I mentioned earlier, I grew up with three father figures. Unfortunately, none of them were spiritual leaders. After I gave my life to Jesus, a fourth father figure came into my life, whom I'll discuss in a minute. Not that they couldn't have been. They were all good men who tried their best in a cruel world, given the tools that were handed down to them by their fathers. I have bits and pieces of all of them that continue to shape a good portion of my personality and character today. From my natural father, my love for great music, my ability to sing and have fun, my joy of cooking, and my gift of hospitality all come from Larry Wayne. Go Gators! From John, my first stepfather, who taught me to work hard, not to be intimidated by those who do things better than you and stay true to who you are and what you can do.

To my third father figure and second stepfather, whose name I will not mention for personal reasons. Some of the roughest and saddest years took place during his reign. Even though there were more negatives than positives, the one thing he taught me that I still use today was a simple thing. When I began to drive at age sixteen, his advice to me was to always carry $50-$100 cash on me. Always have a pen and something to write on. Simple, I know, but for some reason it stuck. To this day, I always have cash on me, I always carry a pen and a notebook, even though today we have phones we can record things on. There is something about writing something down in your own handwriting that I favor.

The fourth father figure was my wife's father, Dan, whom I met before I met my wife. Dan was an usher at the church I was a youth pastor for. Dan was a good man. A hardworking man. A man who had a past and struggled most of his life to be the man everyone thought he could be. Dan was also the first father-figure I had who had a personal relationship with Jesus. Dan was a giver; he taught me that it doesn't always have to be gifts and money. In fact, sometimes the best gift you can give someone is your time and your ears.

Dan had his own struggles with being a father to his children. I watched for almost twenty years as he tried to be a good father to his grown children. What I loved most about Dan is that he became the best grandfather to my son, Kaleb. Dan loved Kaleb and came over unannounced all the time, not to see Sandra or me, but to visit Kaleb. We found out that most of the time, Dan would slip Kaleb a fresh new $100 bill. Every Christmas, Dan would shower Kaleb with gifts. If you asked Kaleb, though, what he loved most about his 'Pawpaw,' it was that he wanted to be around him. Time was the best gift that Dan gave Kaleb. Dan passed away over a decade ago, and Sandra, Kaleb, and I miss him all the time.

As a Spiritual Leader, you set the tone for everything in your children's lives. First, you confirm that God comes first! Having a strong relationship with the Lord and knowing His word gives you the advantage when life happens. The Bible makes it clear that in this life we will have trouble, but through Him we can overcome everything. As a spiritual leader, you give the authority to Jesus Christ. You counsel with the Holy Spirit on decisions and important matters. You establish your house as a house of faith and prayer. Joshua 24:15 states,

"But as for me and my household, we will serve the Lord." This does not mean you are a bully or an authoritarian; it is the opposite. Jesus taught that if you want to be a leader, first learn how to serve.

Understanding what a Spiritual leader possesses guides you into serving your family in a righteous and Godlike manner. This is the opposite of what many children have endured, which is having a religious leader as a father. One who doesn't serve. One who dictates orders, rules, and condemnations. I have friends who grew up in these so-called 'Christian' households, which were more like what Jesus faced in the Pharisees and Sadducees of His day. Sometimes the Devil can twist the word in a man's heart, and it becomes something abusive and detrimental.

I grew up in very worldly homes. God, the Bible, and spiritual things were not discussed. Sometimes I look at it as a blessing. A blessing in the sense that when the time was right, I discovered God on my own terms, read the Word, and developed my own personal relationship with Jesus. On the other hand, I grew up with no moral compass, and sin reigned heavily in my life. I made a ton of bad choices. I treated people terribly. I had no compass and made poor life choices when it came to my future. In that aspect, it would have been nice to have a male in my life who could shake the stupid out of me and show me how God had given me gifts, talents, and treasures to have a successful future. Some of us just take more time than others. I was what they called a 'late bloomer.'

My son Kaleb did not always appreciate my discipline and rules on the things he could and could not do, but I knew that I was building a foundation that would withstand whatever season he would go through in life. Hopefully, when he gets married and has a child, he will understand why I loved and protected him so fiercely. I am sure that as he grows and builds a family, many of those rules he will remember.

The second Pillar we will discuss is that of being a **Strong Tower and a Storehouse**. Proverbs 18:10 states, *"The name of the Lord is a strong tower: the righteous run into it and are safe."* I love the word picture this gives. I just imagine being on a rugged terrain, with a large black storm at my tail. As I look ahead, I see a strong tower built of stone and love. I know if I can get to that tower before the storm hits, I will be safe and protected from the wind, hail, and lightning. This is who God is for us, and as fathers, this is what we need to be for our children.

I am reminded by a strong statement Jesus makes in Matthew 18:5-6 regarding children. *"And whoso shall receive one such little child in my name receives me. But whoso shall offend one of these little ones which believe in me, it were better for him that a millstone were hanged about his neck, and that he were drowned in the depth of the sea."* We as fathers are to be a shelter and a rescue for children, not something that they fear and are mistreated by. Our children should know that when trouble comes, we are the ones they can run to for protection, safety, and counsel.

I remember growing up as kids always comparing our daddies. You would hear someone say, 'My daddy can beat up your daddy.' Such a strange thing to hear now, but there was a sense back in the day of having a strong and protective father. Knowing that if the stuff hit the fan, you could call dad. Children want to feel loved, protected, and provided for. Being able to provide for your children with a roof over their heads, clothes on their back, and food in their bellies goes a long way. Being there day in and day out. I don't know how many times I have seen good men chase money and status. They feel great knowing they have provided a great home, vacations, healthy food, and fancy clothes and things. Down the road, they can't understand why their children want nothing to do with them or are estranged.

They forgot that spending all that time chasing fame and fortune prohibited them from being home and building a personal relationship with their children. There was no tower; it was just a nice house. Children want their fathers to love them and not judge them. They want their fathers to teach them, not preach to them. They want their fathers to be interested in them and spend time on things they are interested in. They want their fathers to guide and protect them, not just let them do whatever they want. As much as we need to be a **Strong Tower** for our children, we also need to be a **Storehouse** for them to come be filled when they need nourishment in all areas of their lives.

Now Merriam-Webster defines the word Storehouse in two main ways: one, a building for storing goods such as provisions. The second meaning is an abundant supply or source. Just like the Word of God is our Storehouse for all Wisdom and Knowledge, a father is to be that same storehouse for their children. Providing the necessary goods, they need growing up, food, clothes, supplies. Fathers also need to provide emotional and intellectual items such as direction, guidance, discipline, support, proper instruction, manners, respect for others and many more.

Children are like sponges so whatever is poured into them they will fill up with. When children grow up in a severely poor household or one where the parents are not parental, they tend to be far behind on the maturity scale both physically and emotionally. Being that Storehouse for our children and providing for their basic needs physically and mentally gives them the proper foundation to fight through the harsh and cruel world they will have to face in their adolescence, teen years and even into their twenties. Matthew 7:9-11 states, *"Which of you, if your son asks for bread, will give him a stone? Or if he asks for a fish, will give him a snake? If you, then, though you are evil, know how to give good gifts to your children, how much more will your Father in heaven give good gifts to those who ask him!"* If we are serving God and understand His goodness toward us, we will instinctively want to provide the very same goodness and needs for our children. Sometimes this goes too far and can become a detriment to children. When parents provide way too much and give their children everything they ask for, they risk teaching their children that life is there to serve them. I have seen many children coming from wealthy families, their upbringing was filled with lavish gifts and overindulgence, and the moment life punches them in the face it is hard for them to understand and get back on their feet. They are simply ill equipped.

Fathers are to provide a safe, secure, and comfortable home. They are to provide food, clothes, and a healthy, moderate lifestyle. Teach their children that you must be willing to work for what you want. Supply them with proper gifts and encouragement as they grow into their adult selves. As we move to the next Pillar, we go into the phase where whatever you are teaching them, you also need to show them or model the proper behavior to them. The third Pillar in building a solid foundation for Fatherhood is to be an excellent **Role Model** for your children. This proves the old mantra that 'More is caught than taught!'

Ephesians 6:4 states, *"Fathers, do not provoke your children to anger by the way you treat them. Rather, bring them up with the discipline and instruction that comes from the Lord."* Children watch everything we do. How we treat our wives, our friends, and our neighbors. Do we gossip about our boss or our coworkers every night we get home? Do we dive into a bottle of beer, wine, or whiskey every night? Do we plop ourselves down on the couch and binge-watch television all night? Do we gain ten pounds a year till we can't see our feet? Our actions speak way more than our words.

Proverbs 22:6 states, *"Train up a child in the way he should go, and when he is old he will not depart from it."* The important moral values and instructions you give and show your children when they are growing will remain as a foundation inside them. That goes for good and bad behaviors. We all have role models growing up; most of them begin as celebrities or athletes. I remember being a baseball pitcher and meeting Nolan Ryan when I was 10 or 11. What a life-changing day that was for me as a ball player. I listened to everything he told me about my stance, my windup, how to hold the ball, and the importance of where and how high my leg is in my windup.

As a father, being a role model who shows your children how to act and behave is crucial. My wife and I both have the gift of hospitality. We would often host events, dinners, and parties at our house. We invited friends and neighbors. We would spend the day cleaning and preparing food and drinks for the party and for our guests. We would serve our guests and make sure they were comfortable in our home. Our son Kaleb was present at most of these events, so he had a bird's eye view of all the things we put into it for it to be enjoyable and a success.

This past Thanksgiving, he was in his own place now and decided to throw a Friendsgiving for his friends and coworkers. He even called me and wanted me to show him how to make our family famous, Hutchinson Chili, which I learned from my father, who learned it from his father. He came over one Sunday, and we made it together. He made it for his Friendsgiving, and it was a big hit. My wife and I were all smiles. He learned that from us. The hosting, the preparing, the serving his guests. We modeled that for him all those years, and now it is his turn when he has children to be the role model of that to them.

What we show our kids, they will retain, whether it be positive or negative. Focus on showing them good habits, good behaviors, and beneficial life skills that will bless them in the future.

The fourth Pillar we will discuss to have strong Father Foundations is to be a **Generational Builder**. Proverbs 13:22 states, *"A good man leaves an inheritance to his children's children, but the wealth of the sinner is stored up for the righteous."* In a perfect world, we will all be rich and leave our children tons of money. We don't live in a perfect world. Most of us live paycheck-to-paycheck, which is another book I could write on the evils of our financial system.

My mother died young and had nothing to give. My father passed, and his assets were about $60,000, split between his four children. That money was spent fairly quickly. So, what else did they leave me? My mother died young, but in the time we had (18 years), the one thing she did for me was that she always believed in me and encouraged my gifts and talents. She was a creative person, and sadly, her tough life squeezed all of that creativity out of her. But I know if she were alive today, the fact that I have pursued my creative side and have written and been in films and television, written and recorded my own songs, written and performed in stage plays, and now writing books, she would be a very proud mother. My father, as I mentioned earlier, left me with a great sense of humor, the desire to have fun, listen to live music, and have a strong group of friends. Did I inherit a million dollars? No! What they did leave me is much more valuable to me. Money can come and go, and without maturity, it can become more of a curse than a blessing.

Should we try to leave monetary gifts? Yes. Will that make all the difference? No! What should we try to leave? A good legacy. Proverbs 22:1 states, *"A good name is to be chosen rather than great riches, loving favor rather than silver and gold."* This is by far one of my favorite scriptures and Proverbs. I think about the people in my life who have mattered the most to me and those whom I remember and emulate; very few of them were wealthy people. Most of them were normal, hard-working, regular folk.

Why do I remember them? They were kind. They were generous. They were supportive. They listened. They encouraged me. They showed up when needed. They counseled when needed. They prayed when I didn't ask. They called when I least expected it. They sowed in me seeds that grew a wealth of knowledge and grace. Some of them had nice cars and fancy houses, but mostly I remember them for the precious and important moments we spent together.

As a good father, it is important that we provide a hope and a future for our children, financially if we can. Just as important is giving them a legacy of living a good and proper life. Having your name spoken well of. Having your reputation held in high regard. Give them real-life tools that will carry them through life, long after you are gone. Faith in God. Love for their family. Strong relationship with friends and peers. If you are a father currently or plan to be one, remember these four pillars: **Spiritual Leader, Strong Tower and Storehouse,**

Role Model, and Generational Builder. It is never too late to correct what you may have done or to prepare for the future children you will have. We will now discuss the final male archetype role that we must learn to become as we walk through life. In the next chapter, we will discuss the importance of being a **Friend.**

Let's continue on our journey!

Chapter 5 Friends Stick Closer than a Brother.

There is one main scripture that I reflect on regarding how to be a **Friend**. That is Proverbs 18:24, which states, *"A man who has friends must himself be friendly, but there is a friend who sticks closer than a brother."* I quote this scripture frequently, from the pulpit and when having men's Bible studies. I love this because it presents two key facts: one, you make more friends when you are friendly. The second and crucial fact is that many times, family doesn't treat you as well as they should. Sometimes friends become even closer than family. Some live far away from their family, so friends in many scenarios become family to us and even to our children.

I moved to Texas from Florida before I got married and had my son, Kaleb. As he grew up, he didn't see my family but maybe once a year, if that. He grew up with friends coming to the house. My son refers to many of my good friends as 'Uncles.' He has Uncle Wardlow, Uncle Bravo, Uncle Inappropriate (not in the bad way), and others. As you show yourself to be friendly, courteous, respectful, and kind, you will attract people into your life. They may become closer than your own family members. They do not replace family members (unless they need to!)

Our lives nowadays are split into at least three quadrants: our family life, our work life, and our social life. In today's world, our social lives even exist on our devices. When I was growing up, you had to belong to a bowling league or be on some sports team or recreational club to have a social life. You met people outside the home and work, and in a physical scenario. You talked over food, drink, and activities. In this chapter, we will discuss the four pillars that make for a good Friend.

Those include:

1) **Being Purposeful.**

2) **Be Authentic.**

3) **Have Commitment.**

4) **Use Two ears and One Mouth.**

Once again, I am authoring this book in the fall of 2025, and our world is unfortunately a digital world now. Most people are hermits and communicate through digital texts, pictures, and music. If that wasn't bad enough, the demonic powers that be that released the COVID psyop, purposefully wanted the world to be in fear and stay at home. For a good part of the population who worked. We were not created to be isolated, alone, or afraid of each other. Here is a hint! Any social and mainstream media storyline that wants you to be afraid of the outdoors, each other, because of politics, religion, or the color of our skin is a demonic agenda. God created us to walk together in the garden and meet with Him in the cool of the day.

You want to have friends and life-long friends as well, then you must be "**Purposeful!**" What do I mean? I have what I would call about five really close friends. I'm not lucky! It's on purpose! Each one of them I have a different relationship with each one of them, meaning we communicate in the exact way that is beneficial to the other. How did I do that? I purposefully make sure every month to leave time out of my busy schedule to meet one-on-one with them or host a fun event where most, if not all of them, can attend. I give them plenty of notice when we get together, and I give them the option of choosing the place they like.

I reach out! I make the effort! I make the time! I hear people say all the time, "I haven't seen my friends or family in so long." Which I always reply with, "When's the last time you met them for coffee or something to eat?" Which they reply, "I wish I had the time." These are the same people who tell me they just spend eight hours binge watching the new show on Netflix! They were being 'Purposeful,' but just for watching their new show!

We live in a cruel, harsh world. We need each other. The Devil has provided the devices and the distractions to keep us alone! As a friend, a good friend, it is my responsibility to do regular check-ups on those I love. In doing so, I get checked up on as well. How do I purposefully build a relationship with the people I desire to have in my life? I meet for breakfast, lunch, a beer, or hang out somewhere. Every quarter, I host an event at my house, usually a professional wrestling event or some sort of movie double feature. I sent out the invitation. I let them know I'm cooking, and they just need to bring their own beverage or dessert and show up.

As men, it is important that we surround ourselves with like-minded men, especially those who have the same faith and belief system as we do. Be careful, especially if you are a God-fearing man, to surround yourself with other men who are living for the Devil. I have seen pastors and good friends let a wolf in the hen house, and the next thing you know, the pastor is having affairs or robbing from his congregation. Being purposeful means, you select who is to be in your life with you and how you choose to spend time with those individuals. As the Bible says, show yourself friendly if you want to be a friend.

The next Pillar we will discuss on how to be a Friend is to **Be Authentic**. I live in the Dallas/Fort Worth metroplex. I will admit that, probably other than Los Angeles and New York City, Dallas has the third most fake individuals in the United States. The metroplex is very materialistic. We have tons of churches and a dozen or more mega churches, but the amount of plastic and paint these people are covered in makes me very weary sometimes. Status is important in this area. Because of that, many people hide who they truly are and put on a façade to try to make it in this harsh jungle of the DFW!

I know that we live in a world where it seems everybody needs to take a selfie and post it to social media. Every minimal event is a life-changing moment on the X or Instagram highway. It feels like most people are playing a role. Do we really represent our authentic selves anymore? One of my favorite scriptures in the Bible comes from Matthew 16:13-17, which states, *"Now, when Jesus came into the coasts of Caesarea Philippi, he asked his disciples, saying, Whom do men say that I the Son of man am? And they said, Some say that thou art John the Baptist: some, Elias; and others, Jeremias, or one of the prophets. He saith unto them, But who say ye that I am? And Simon Peter answered and said, Thou art the Christ, the Son of the living God. And Jesus answered and said unto him, Blessed art thou, Simon Barjona: for flesh and blood hath not revealed it unto thee, but my Father which is in heaven."*

I love this because even Christ himself wanted to take the temperature of who His disciples perceived Him to be. This should be a yearly exercise for you to ask those closest to you who they think you are. To see if what you are projecting to those around you is who you truly are. My day job is that of a mild-mannered business broker. I help business owners sell their companies for maximum value and retire. In the beginning stages of discussing the sale with the owner, I always let them know that they need to reveal what we call "The Good, The Bad & The Ugly," which we stole from that great Western Film.

The truth is that when we go through due diligence on a company we are selling, between the banks and the lawyers, anything that can be uncovered will be uncovered. It is so much easier when we know in the beginning what red flags or obstacles we will face in the process of the sale. You should be the same way with your friendships. You should be presenting your authentic self to those with whom you wish to have a relationship. Especially if you want it to last. We reveal in our first meeting that our firm is a Christian Firm. We believe in Jesus, which means to us that we are High Integrity, High Transparency, and High Confidentiality, and we will strive for the best and fairest deal for all parties.

This doesn't mean you have to be a completely open book and blab out all your life to everyone. It just means that you present your truest self. Be open about your beliefs. Be open about your political stances. Be open about how you want to be treated. Be open about things you will say no to. My small group of guys that I hang out with the most are not bashful about the guilty pleasures we enjoy. We often get together for Karaoke Night. We often get together to watch a professional Wrestling event. We often get together and do a double-feature movie night. On occasion, we will go out to dinner or to a brewery and just visit.

Find your tribe and keep them. One by being purposeful and by being your authentic self. This doesn't mean you will not have differences, different belief systems, or different political affiliations. What it means is that you are all open and honest about who you are and find a middle ground to do life together. We are living in a demonic time where our political figures and celebrities are pushing the lie that if we believe differently, we can't come together. The Devil is a liar! The truth is that more opposites attract than similar personalities.

My wife and I have been married for 27 years, and we have just as many things in common as we do things that are opposite. We have learned to adapt and adjust to the things that are different because we respect each other's authentic selves. The other thing that keeps us together is the third pillar we will discuss on being a Friend and that is **Having Commitment**!

A faithful friend, a faithful spouse, and a faithful parent are worth their weight in Gold. We live in a world where trends set the pace. People change at the drop of a hat based on what they believe on their social media platforms. Just try to recall all the psyops, the political elite, Hollywood, and the music industries have shoved down our throats. All the different symbols and flags that you must change on your social media cover. They seem committed to a cause until the next programmed social discourse begins, and then they quickly shift to the next thing they are commanded to care about.

You can see this even in the church, all the denominational splits, all the spiritual movements of the month. People in general have a hard time standing on a foundation for too long. It may be because of the modern technological world we live in, where everything is temporary. We watch 30-90 second clips on our phones. We want to binge-watch a show in half a day.

We hate having to wait a whole week for the next episode. Now people won't even go to the store or spend the time cooking; they will call a service to bring them food that costs more and isn't as hot as it could be.

How in the world will we stay committed in our relationships? I want you to grab something to write on and write with. This only applies to someone who is above twenty-five. Write down on a piece of paper the individuals in your life that you speak with or visit with monthly besides your family. List them on the paper. Now, write down next to their names how long you have been in a friendship with them. Hopefully, you have one or two that have a number higher than 7. If so, then you can say that you are in a committed friendship.

If all of them are under 7 it means three things: One, you move a lot. Two, you are a hermit and like to be alone. Three, you are not being purposeful, being your authentic self or staying committed. I know it is hard. We live busy complicated lives. We have many more priorities than we used to it seems. Between work, eating and sleeping, how many hours do we really have in a day?

I have heard so many excuses from so many people, I get it!

When I talk to someone who states that they feel alone or feel that they do not have anyone in their life, I usually ask them some questions. How often do you reach out to others? How many times have you invited someone for coffee or a meal? How many events have you hosted at your place or somewhere in your city? Do you belong to any social clubs in your area? Do you go to any networking meetings to meet new people?

Most people think that there is some magic genie somewhere that is just going to send people your way. As the Bible says, if you want friends, you need to be friendly. It is tough sometimes, I admit it. Do I get tired of being the one who always reaches out? Do I get tired of being the one who always hosts the event? Do I wish my phone would ring more regularly with a 'How's it going?' Yes, to all the above. It can be cumbersome to be the only committed one in the bunch sometimes. The reward of that commitment is when I look at my list of names on my list and every one of them is over 10 years, some now 40 years of friendship. My commitment keeps my calendar full.

Hopefully, one day, when Jesus brings me home to Heaven, there will be a few people at my funeral who will wax poetically about what a good and faithful friend I was and how I made a difference in their lives. I plan on standing at their funeral if they go before me and say the same thing. Commitment is crucial. Let your, yes, be yes, and your no be no! Keep your visits regular and personal. It is easy to have a text friend or a social media friend. It takes work and commitment to have a friend who meets you in person. That comes with a higher level of love, respect, and appreciation. I promise you, the more you meet in person, the longer that friendship will endure.

As a business broker, we understand the magic that happens when we get a buyer and seller in person, not once but on multiple occasions. It breeds familiarity, trust, and a bond that is harder to break. This is why I am purposeful in reaching out. Having coffee, lunch, or a cold beer with my friends. This is why I go to the store, cook a good meal, and invite my bro's over to the house for fun. As I do these things, I also practice the last pillar that is important to being a Friend that sticks closer than a brother, and that is to use **Two Ears and One Mouth**!

James 1:19 states, *"Understand this, my dear brothers and sisters: You must all be quick to listen, slow to speak, and slow to get angry. Human anger does not produce the righteousness God desires."* We live in a world of Chatty Kathy Dolls. Everyone loves to hear their own voice. Their own opinions. Gossip is the number one sin in the world. People can talk! People pull their own strings, too. We all have friends, family members, or co-workers who talk like Niagara Falls flows. There is no turning off that flow, and there is no way you will get a word in.

To be a good friend, don't be like that! A good friend listens. A good friend comments when needed. A good friend advises when warranted. It is an art for sure. The art of listening should be taught in school and college. There is a huge advantage in listening. People tend to let things slip out, that they normally, would keep hidden. When people get on a roll talking and emotions get high, they usually will say the quiet part out loud. If you are trying to interrupt and get your two cents in, you might miss the most vital information of the conversation and your meeting.

I am a man who keeps most things pretty close to the chest. I can be a man of few words. I am also a very passionate man and have strong beliefs on certain subjects. Depending on where the conversation goes, I can be as quiet as a church mouse or as loud as a fire engine. To be a good and faithful friend, you will need to listen more and speak less. Ask the right questions. Read the room. Each of my friends deals with different issues in their own personal lives. When I'm around them, I pay attention to their body language. I listen to the tone of their voice. I make a mental note of the things they laugh at or the little comments they make at certain subjects. When I have discernment that they need to vent, I will then purposefully ask them for coffee, breakfast, or to meet for a beer.

There will be seasons when you need to sit and listen to your friends tell all the things they are dealing with personally, professionally, and spiritually. If you sow your time and your ears to listen, when your season comes to need a friend to listen, hopefully they will be there to return the favor. A friend who sticks closer than a brother means you put other people's needs in front of your own, which is hard in this day and age of narcissism. We live in a day and age where the Devil is wreaking havoc on political correctness and the like of wokeism.

Unfortunately, the education system and new parents are raising up generations who cannot be corrected or hear a harsh word or criticism. Everyone gets a trophy and a timeout room to deal with events, memes, and posts that hurt their feelings way too much. I never received a cozy room when I grew up. The mean words spoken over me, the chastising, the middle fingers and shoves in the hallway were all life's way of teaching me to grow up and grow a spine.

If I had a bully challenge me to a fight after school, I showed, did my best, and took whatever licks came my way. I stood my ground, though, tried to get a few jabs in, and stood up to the bully. I didn't get to hide behind social media posts or socially acceptable identities. We had guns back then and knives; we were all just mature enough to handle it with fists. I know people now are more sensitive; it is due to the bubble wrap that was placed around their lives. When I was growing up, you would never be cancelled for your opinion or if you used a word that needed to be used. The Devil has softened the sheep.

It is even more crucial now to listen. I am a Pastor, and I work with the younger generation. I must listen to them and hear what they are afraid of. Sadly, there is a ton of fear in our society. More triggers than there used to be. Despite having more convenience and more information available, it doesn't seem to fortify anyone. Maybe there is too much data!

I count myself blessed. I have a group of great, faithful, positive friends in my life. I give God the Glory! I also know that it was a concerted effort on my part. I am a firm believer in the four pillars we discussed. **Be purposeful! Be authentic! Have commitment! Use two ears and one mouth**! It is not a quick and easy process. It takes time to build quality friendships. As you grow older, it becomes important to have a group of friends around you to help and support you in times of need. There are super awesome families who are always there, but I find this to be the exception rather than the norm.

Remember the exercise we did, writing down the list of friends and how long the relationship has been. The next exercise is to go back to that list and see if there are some that need to be improved. Maybe you need to spend more time with one or two to grow the relationship. There might even be a relationship you are holding on to that you need to let go of. There may be someone who needs the maturity, grace, and compassion you can provide for them. Just like in marriage, it is always good to continually take the temperature of the relationship. Now that we have made it through the four male archetypes and models God has for us, let us spend time reviewing. Let's continue on this journey!

Chapter 6 Become a Mature Man

Start a real conversation with God and yourself. Ask God how you are doing in these four distinct roles. Be open to the Holy Spirit to show you where you can improve, where you need to repent, and how to become the mature man He has designed you to be. I'm in my mid-fifties, and my father passed away three years ago. My father-in-law passed away eleven years ago. My role as a **Son** is still with my Father in Heaven. If you are still young and have an earthly father or father-in-law, strive to be a good son. We all have family issues; some are terrible, some stay around because of our pride. To be a good son, ask God what He would have you do in your relationship with the earthly fathers He has provided for you. Remember, God put you in the family you are in. For a reason as well!

If there is a male in your life who is older and wiser than you but is not a biological or marital father to you, ask God how you are to be with such a person. I have had many men in my life who were older mentors for me, whom God used to father me in one way or another. It was my charge to honor them and sit under their wisdom and authority. Keep your eyes open for God to use mature and good men to guide you through life. One day He may call on you to do the same!

Are you married? Are you single? Either way, strive to learn what it means to be a good **Husband**. I have been married for 27 years, and I'm still growing as a husband. There are still areas I am allowing God to help me with. Do I fail? Absolutely! We are human. We also should have a desire to improve and be sanctified in Christ. That takes time and doesn't always feel good. Being a good husband is an offering to God. Jesus is our groom, and He is a good husband to His bride.

If you are single and desire to get married, read God's word and know what will be required of you to be a good husband. Being a good husband is just as difficult as finding a good woman to be your wife, but when you do, cherish it. Fight for it! Understand your role as a good provider, a disciplinarian, a decision maker, and the spiritual head of the family. Don't let the emotions of lust and love intoxicate you and manipulate you to get married when you are not prepared or ready to be a good husband. Being in a committed marriage is hard enough; when it starts with fleeting emotions, when storms come, the ship sinks.

It is hard enough not to be spiritually ready to be a husband; being a **father** is just as difficult. The Devil's number one enemy is a Godly father. Being the spiritual head of the household. A strong male figure who leads righteously and disciplines righteously is a strong tower against the enemy's plans. A good father leads with integrity, self-discipline, Godly wisdom, and discernment. As we mentioned earlier, most criminals and individuals who struggle with drugs and alcohol come from a single-parent home, specifically a fatherless home.

A Godly father's role is to lay the proper foundation of faith, hope, and love for each member of the family. To instill a proper sense of community and fellowship with others. To keep a peaceful and organized home. To teach and train your children in the way they should go, as the Bible advises. To learn from your mistakes and to model to your children to admit shortcomings, repent, and allow God to help you grow stronger.

Keep the world from manipulating and stealing the joy from your household. Keep vain arguments like religion and politics at bay. Be a good host and show your children that family, friends, and community are important, and it is God's design to do life together with others. Be a good **Friend**!

Help others in need when it is in your power to do so. Expand your influence and help build and grow with a group of friends. Be a source of love for your friends. A safe place where they can confide in you and share their heart. Be a leader and help lead other men in their God-designed roles. The Bible refers to iron sharpening iron, as a good friend helps sharpen each other in the Word of God. Make sure you, as a healthy reader of the Bible, are available in season and out to give an encouraging word to your friends.

The challenge of being a mature man of God is to thrive in the four roles of being a **Son, Husband, Father, and Friend**. A balancing act that will not come easy. It is crucial to keep yourself in the Word. To make time for prayer and conversation with God. To seek God's divine will and purpose for your life. To allow God to shape and mold you into the vessel he created you to be. Do not be swayed or turned by every wind of doctrine or false views that run contrary to God's word. Put on the armor of God each day. Fight the good fight. Be a good steward of the gifts and talents God has bestowed upon you from birth. As a mature man of God, your final task is to do what God commanded us to do, and that is to make disciples.

Chapter 7 Make Disciples

The last command Jesus gave before he ascended into the clouds was from Matthew 28:19-20, which states, *"Therefore go and make disciples of all nations, baptizing them in the name of the Father and of the Son and of the Holy Spirit, and teaching them to obey everything I have commanded you. And surely, I am with you always, to the very end of the age."* A clear instruction for us to go and do what He did. Two main things from this passage I'd like to point out are *make disciples,* and *surely, I am with you always, to the very end of the age.* Hopefully, as you read through this book, God will reveal to you every area as a son, husband, father, and friend that you need to grow and mature in.

As you work on the pillars in each archetype, understand that the source for all your wisdom and strength will come from the Lord Jesus Christ. It is difficult to grow. It hurts to mature in life. With each step in a positive direction, you can give Glory to God as He walks alongside you through all of it. When you begin to activate your talents and giftings as a son, husband, father, and friend, do what Jesus has commanded us to do and make disciples. Teach others what God has taught you.

I meet with people who have the desire to write. Whether it is books, plays, or screenplays, we all have a creative spark somewhere inside of us. We have a story to tell; it may be fiction, but underneath are truths we want to express. I enjoy mentoring and showing others how to successfully build, create, and write their stories. I have embraced the gifts that God has given me and do my best to give back and sow into others so they can experience the beauty of writing a story. As you grow in your maturity as a man of God, make sure you take time to help others who desire to grow in these four areas.

As men, it is crucial that we get together. I know many times it is for fun and enjoyment, but we must also spend quality time with each other. Quality in the sense that we allow each other to open up and discuss what is really going on inside us. How is our heart? How is our health? How is our walk with God? These are crucial issues that Jesus wants us to help each other with. As we mentioned before, iron sharpens iron! Men tend to keep things close to the chest and not discuss the hard stuff with which they are dealing. We were probably taught by our fathers to suck it up and move on!

There is a time and a place to be silent, but there is also a time when you need to let someone know you need help. The Holy Spirit was sent to us as our comforter. Those of us who have the indwelling of the Holy Spirit, it is our Holy duty to be our brother's keeper. Don't forget to refill your soul and Spirit as well. In some season you may be the one sowing and giving over and over to others. Many times, this causes us to be drained or empty. We may grow weary in well-doing, as the Bible says. Make sure when you need encouragement and refilling, you call your brothers who can sow into you and bless you with their time, talent, and treasure.

So how can we make disciples? As our first pillar, a friend suggested 'Be Purposeful!' Are you a part of a small men's group? If yes, continue. If no, find one or ask the Lord if you should start one. Does the church you attend have one? Check! Maybe you are not attending church; if so, find a men's group and attend that as part of your fellowshipping with others. Maybe God will lead you to do what I did and host a "Grown

Ass Men" night! If you have a house and a backyard with a grill, invite your friends and co-workers over once a quarter and hang out.

I have been doing my GAM (Grown Ass Men) nights for almost two decades now, and it is an exciting time to just be dudes and discuss real-life stuff. Maybe you find three or four guys, and you do outings like a movie, ballgame, or dinner once a quarter. Ask the Lord if it is something you should begin or suggest to a group. I have remarkable stories from our meetings. There have been important moments when somebody opened up and really needed the love and input that the other men were able to provide.

The point is to be active! Do something! Make disciples! Duplicate what God has done in you. I promise you, as you grow in God and share what God has done in you, He will continue to richly bless you. I hope you have enjoyed this book and have gained some insight into what it means to be a Mature Man of God and to grow into your role as a **Son, Husband, Father, and Friend!** If you would like to grow in other areas in your life, I recommend two other books I have written, *The Puzzle of You and I* and *The Whack Life*.

The Puzzle of You and I discusses the delicate process of solving some of life's toughest puzzles. We discuss how to organize and put together your Spiritual, Physical, Emotional, Relational, and Financial puzzles. Find a good balance in your life and find the picturesque life you have been envisioning. *The Whack Life* is a small book on how to change your life and accomplish your dreams by understanding the power of goals, goal setting, and achieving those goals. Both these books are a terrific addition to this book and will give you a well-rounded approach to improving your body, soul, and spirit.

I know this may seem overwhelming. Especially with all the information provided. Good things usually take time. Tackle one thing at a time. Ask God which area you should focus on first and concentrate on that. If you are not a husband or a father yet, then focus on being the best son and friend you can now. Study what it means to be a husband and father and prepare yourself for when God provides that special someone for you. I know we live in a busy world these days, even though we should have more time because of technology. I would suggest to you to block off some time for yourself in the next weeks and months and focus on the pillars provided and read the bible.

If it helps, get a journal to track your thoughts, concerns and changes you make in your life. Find a faithful friend who can come alongside you and encourage your journey. Someone who you can be open with and talk to. Someone who you can share your fears with. You do not have to be on this journey alone. Beside the Holy Spirit being with you, God will provide you with friends or family members to walk along side of you as well.

Remember in all things seek God! Be thankful for all His gifts and blessings! Be patient! Know how to thrive and strive in life; both will happen. You were put on this Earth for a purpose, and praise God. Seek His will for your life. Read his Word! Be a light for someone. Continue your journey! May God give you wisdom, discernment, and understanding in all things. May He prosper you and give you good health!

Until next time, keep reading!

The following Books can be purchased on Amazon.com.

"The Puzzle of You and I"

Written by Todd Hutchinson

Copyright 2025©

TKS Venture Holdings, LLC Publishing

"The Whack Life"

Written by Todd Hutchinson

Copyright 2025©

TKS Venture Holdings, LLC Publishing

"100 Things I'm Going to do This Year"

Written by Todd Hutchinson

Copyright 2025©

TKS Venture Holdings, LLC Publishing

www.ingramcontent.com/pod-product-compliance
Lightning Source LLC
Chambersburg PA
CBHW071204090426
42736CB00030B/3104